How Is the Weather?

sunny

rainy

windy

snowy

cloudy

foggy

cold

hot

How's the weather?

It's sunny.

How's the weather?

It's rainy.

How's the weather?

It's windy.

How's the weather?

It's snowy.

How's the weather?

It's cold, very cold.

Let's learn more about Australia.

Meat pie